Dangerous Floods

Carol Kim

Lerner Publications • Minneapolis

Lerner Publications Company
An imprint of Lerner Publishing Group, Inc.
241 First Avenue North
Minneapolis, MN 55401 USA

For reading levels and more information, look up this title at www.lernerbooks.com.

Main body text set in Billy Infant Regular. Typeface provided by SparkType.

Library of Congress Cataloging-in-Publication Data

Names: Kim, Carol, author.
Title: Dangerous floods / Carol Kim.
Description: Minneapolis : Lerner Publications, [2022] | Series: Lightning bolt books - earth in danger | Includes bibliographical references and index. | Audience: Ages 6–9 | Audience: Grades 2–3 | Summary: "What happens when floods rise higher and happen more frequently? Many areas are dealing with more floods because of climate change. Learn what causes floods and how to stay safe when floods get dangerous"— Provided by publisher.
Identifiers: LCCN 2021022463 (print) | LCCN 2021022464 (ebook) | ISBN 9781728441450 (library binding) | ISBN 9781728447940 (paperback) | ISBN 9781728444833 (ebook)
Subjects: LCSH: Floods—Juvenile literature.
Classification: LCC GB1399 .K53 2022 (print) | LCC GB1399 (ebook) | DDC 363.34/93—dc23

LC record available at https://lccn.loc.gov/2021022463
LC ebook record available at https://lccn.loc.gov/2021022464

Manufactured in the United States of America
1-49916-49759-8/2/2021

Table of Contents

Water Everywhere

Rain keeps falling and falling. The water in streams and rivers rises higher and higher. They begin to overflow. Water covers the ground and spreads.

Water rushes down sidewalks and roads. Buildings and homes fill with water. This is a flood.

These houses in South Carolina were flooded after a heavy rain in 2015.

This flood in Louisiana happened because of a hurricane.

Most floods are caused by very heavy rainfall. Dam breaks or melting snow can also cause floods. Sometimes strong storm winds push seawater inland.

FLASH FLOOD AREA

NEXT 3 MILES

Signs point out areas where flash floods may happen.

Floods usually happen slowly, over hours or days. But some happen quickly, in only minutes. These are flash floods.

The Power of Water

Floodwater currents can be very strong. Water flowing just 4 miles (6.4 km) an hour can move boulders 5 feet (1.5 m) across.

The water can carry away cars and even homes. People and animals may be swept away.

Water can lift and move heavy objects easily.

Floodwater reached the ceiling of this house and caused damage.

Floodwater sometimes gets into buildings. The water ruins everything inside and outside. It can also damage bridges and roads.

Floods happen everywhere in the world. They are the most common natural disaster. Floods cause more than $40 billion in damage each year.

A flood can damage all the buildings in its path.

Preparing for Floods

Scientists called hydrologists study floods. They try to predict when a flood may be coming. They track water in rivers and in the ground.

Floodwater from hail and rain pools on this road.

When rainfall is heavy and the ground is already wet, flooding is more likely. Flood warnings can go out hours or even days in advance.

Flash floods are much harder to predict. They can happen very quickly, with little warning. Flash floods are the most dangerous type of flood.

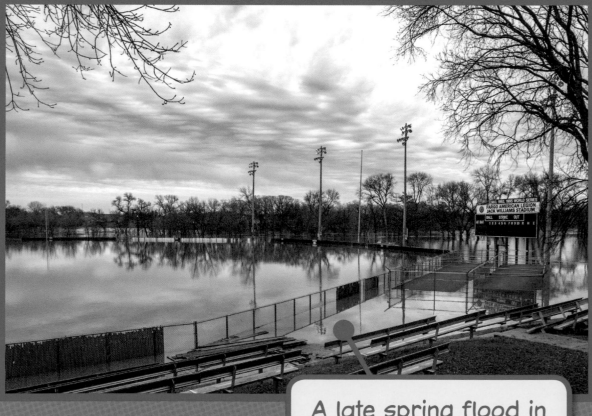

A late spring flood in Fargo, North Dakota

Miami, Florida, flooded during Hurricane Irma in 2017.

Climate change can make floods worse. Warmer air makes hurricanes drop more rain. Melting polar ice raises sea levels and causes more coastal flooding.

15

Flood Safety

Floods are dangerous. If evacuation orders are issued, be sure to follow them. Move to higher ground to be safe.

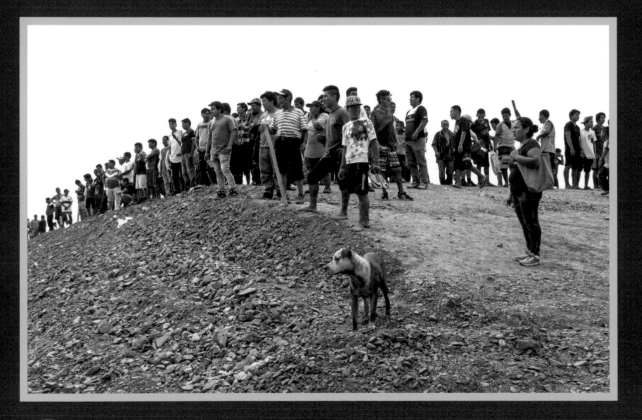

This car was swept away by floodwaters during a tropical storm.

Never drive or walk into floodwaters. Cars can be carried away in 2 feet (0.6 m) of water or less. Just 6 inches (15 cm) of moving water can knock a person over.

Put together an emergency kit with food, water, and medicine. Include flashlights, batteries, and a first aid kit.

Emergency kits should contain only food that won't spoil.

Floods can be scary. But if you know what to do during a flood, you and your family will stay safe.

I Survived a Flash Flood

When Sarah Owen started hiking along the Paria Canyon in Utah, the weather was clear. But then it began to rain. Owen was near a river. She knew a flash flood could happen. She spotted a small cave high up on the canyon wall and climbed up into it.

The river quickly rose to within a few feet of her cave. For several hours, she was trapped. When the water level finally fell, Owen hiked back to safety.

Flood Facts

- Experts believe floodwaters can flow at speeds of up to 67 miles (108 km) an hour.

- The record for rainfall from one storm was set by Hurricane Harvey in 2017. The storm dumped more than 60 inches (152 cm) of rain over Nederland, Texas, northeast of Houston.

- The worst flood in history happened in 1931 in China. Water from the Yangtze and Huai Rivers covered 34,000 square miles (88,060 sq. km) of land.

- The Atacama Desert gets less than 0.2 inches (0.5 cm) of rain a year. But in March 2015, 1 to 2 inches (2.5 to 5 cm) of rain fell in twenty-four hours. This caused flash floods and mudslides in the area.

Glossary

climate change: changes in weather patterns driven by human activity

current: the movement of water in one direction

dam: a barrier that holds back water

evacuation: leaving an area to avoid danger

flash flood: a sudden rush of water into an area, usually with no warning

hurricane: a strong storm with heavy rain and high winds

hydrologist: a scientist who studies water and the water cycle

inland: away from the sea

polar ice: ice found in the North and South Poles

Learn More

Alderman, Christine Thomas. *Floods*. Mankato, MN: Black Rabbit, 2021.

National Geographic Kids: Flood
https://kids.nationalgeographic.com/science/article/flood

National Weather Service: Weather Science
https://www.weather.gov/owlie/science_kt

Schaefer, Lola. *Dangerous Hurricanes*. Minneapolis: Lerner Publications, 2022.

Suen, Anastasia. *Floods*. Mankato, MN: Amicus, 2021.

Weather Wiz Kids: Rain and Floods
https://www.weatherwizkids.com/weather-rain.htm

Index

Photo Acknowledgments

Image credits: Virginia State Parks/flickr (CC BY 2.0), p. 4; U.S. Air Force photo by Staff Sgt. Douglas Ellis/flickr, p. 5; ccpixx photography/Shutterstock.com, p. 6; Famartin/Wikimedia Commons (CC BY-SA 4.0), p. 7; Marie Shearin Images/Shutterstock.com, p. 8; Roypix/ Shutterstock.com, p. 9; Brian Nolan/Shutterstock.com, p. 10; David Fine/FEMA/Wikimedia Commons, p. 11; USDA photo by Scott Bauer/flickr (CC BY 2.0), p. 12; sassy1902/E+/Getty Images, p. 13; USDA Photo by Lance Cheung/flickr (CCO 1.0), p. 14; Warren Faidley/The Image Bank/Getty Images, p. 15; AP Photo/Rodrigo Abd, p. 16; Marvin Nauman/FEMA/Wikimedia Commons, p. 17; LifestyleVisuals/iStock/Getty Images, p. 18; FatCamera/iStock/Getty Images, p. 19.

Cover: South Carolina Air National Guard/Senior Airman Megan Floyd/169th Fighter Wing Public Affairs (CCO 1.0).